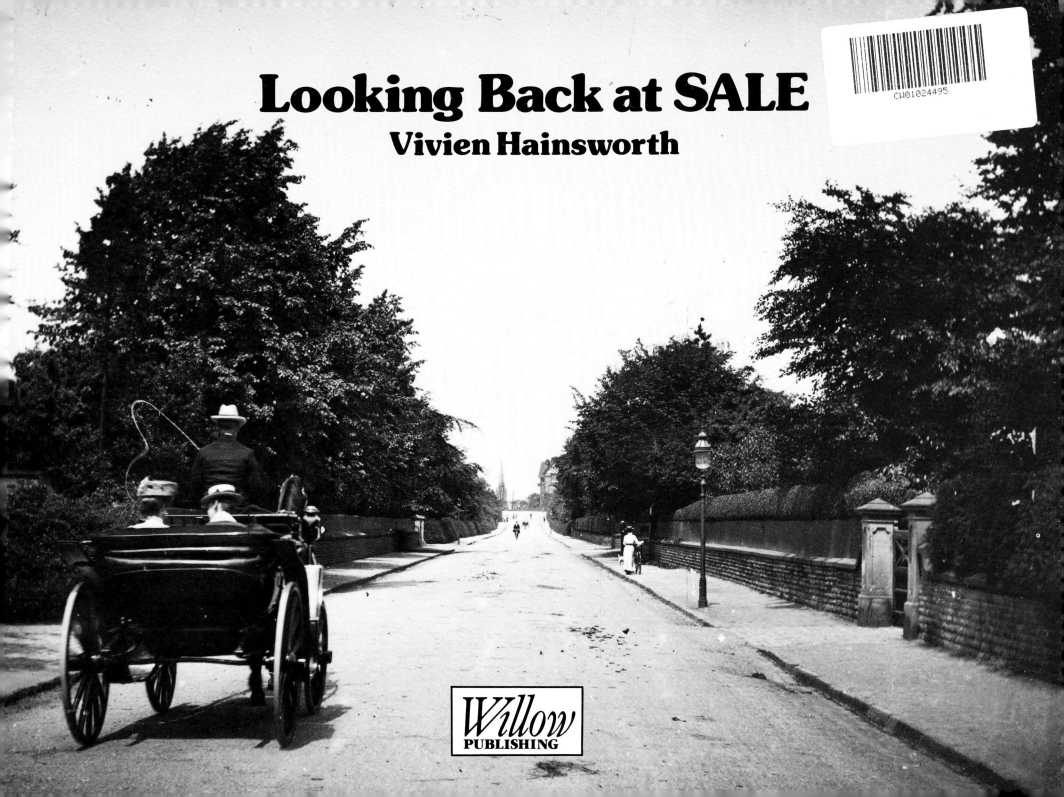

Looking Back at SALE
Vivien Hainsworth

Willow PUBLISHING

Acknowledgments

I would like to thank Mr J W H Watters, Borough Librarian of Trafford for kindly allowing me to reproduce many of the enclosed photographs and giving me access to many historical items, I must also thank many people in Sale and Ashton-upon-Mersey who have donated photographs or who have in some manner provided useful information. These people include Mr Goulding, Principal Engineer for Trafford. Mrs D Vickers, Mr Ledger, Mr T Marriott-Moore, Mrs Reece, Mr A Foulkes, Mr Royle and Mr S Harris, an ex mayor of Sale and many people who wish to remain anonymous. Miss C M Whittaker, the Garner family and His Honour Judge D Bailey greatly assisted my efforts by allowing me to borrow some exquisite family photographs, while John Rylands University Library and Whitbreads Brewery kindly gave me access to some of their records. Mr J Jones of Sale who is now unfortunately deceased will be remembered for having the patience to recall some of his early memories of Sale which in turn helped in the compilation of this work. Finally if it had not been for Mr N V Swain and Mr E P Lee this book would never have been written. Several years ago both gentlemen stimulated my interest in local history and in particular Mr Swain has been a constant source of inspiration and information ever since.

Vivien Hainsworth 1983

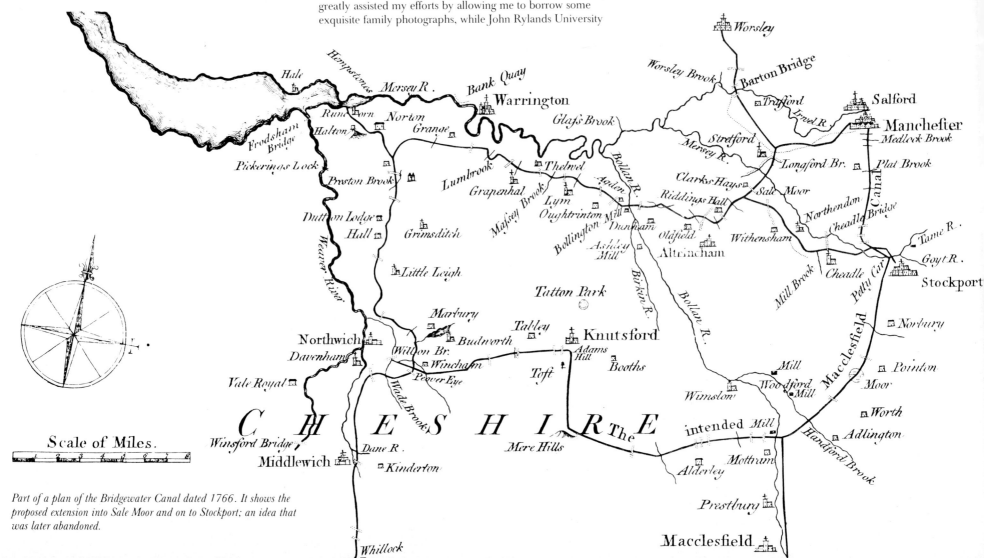

Part of a plan of the Bridgewater Canal dated 1766. It shows the proposed extension into Sale Moor and on to Stockport; an idea that was later abandoned.

School Road looking in the direction of Washway Road, c 1890's. Boots the Chemist stands on the site of the Wesleyan Chapel (left).

Introduction

When passing through Sale today there is perhaps little evidence to suggest that the locality possesses any historical origins outside the twentieth century. One of its most singular features today though and one that might easily be overlooked, is the main highway of Cross Street and Washway Road; the antecedent of which was the main Roman road of Watling Street. This major Roman artery stretched from London to the north of England, where in the north west it connected the fortress of Deva or Chester with the auxiliary fort of Mancunium or Manchester. In this capacity Sale featured in Roman Britain merely as another part of a wild desolate region containing a military route.

Charles Bertram and the Roman Fort

Over the years there have been various papers written on the subject of a Roman fort having been situated in Ashton-upon-Mersey but these were based on spurius information. Somewhere between 1747 and 1757 a man called Charles Bertram of London and later Copenhagen, conceived the idea of attaining fame and fortune by producing a series of literary forgeries and to this end selected the famous antiquarian, Dr. William Stukeley to be the unfortunate person who would unwittingly assist him in this deed. So in 1747 he started writing to Dr. Stukeley and in the course of their correspondence just happened to mention that a friend of his possessed a manuscript work on the subject of Roman antiquities; a work written by a monk, one Richard of Westminster. In a spirit of eager anticipation Dr. Stukeley replied, pressing Bertram to try and obtain the manuscript with which the latter willingly complied, agreeing to provide a facsimile of a few lines of the document and later a map of Roman sites. Bertram's forgeries were so good and his historical knowledge of the period so well informed that his material was readily accepted by contemporary historians, culminating in it being accepted and promulgated by Dr. Stukeley. It is hard to estimate the disservice Bertram did to the study of Roman Britain as many future historians perpetuated his false information which was not fully discovered until the 1860's. Consequently this fraudulent material is still evident even in the first edition of the Ordnance Survey map of Sale in 1842 which shows the location of a Roman fort in Ashton-on-Mersey, marked as 'FINES MAXIMAE ET FLAVIAE'; and it is also evident in some of the contemporary nineteenth century histories of Cheshire.

Early History

From purely etymological evidence it is thought that the word Sale might be of Anglo-Saxon derivation as it only has one syllable. Dane Road on the other hand, or Dene Road or Lane as it is shown on some maps, was a term used in the same period to denote a valley and of course today the road still skirts the remains of the alluvial Mersey Valley. Unfortunately as yet, there is no textual or site evidence to substantiate this theory. Again Sale is not mentioned in the Domesday Book either, though this may not necessarily mean that the area did not support the occasional dwelling.

The first tangible piece of evidence for any human settlement in Sale is in the form of a twelfth century document in which Thomas de Hyde made a grant of a portion of land in

Sale Township to Henry de Trafford, the rent charged being an iron barbed arrow. During this period Sale and Ashton-upon-Mersey would have been generally inhospitable places, the major part probably consisting of tracts of waste and areas of forest and moorland, hence the name, Sale Moor. The Mersey valley would most probably have been a treacherously swampy region periodically flooding the surrounding lands. Occasional small dwellings might have been dotted around in the less desolate areas, certainly centreing round the old church of St. Martin in Ashton-upon-Mersey, by the fourteenth century.

Moving on to the seventeenth century, Sale had become a farming and weaving community with garthweb weaving being predominant. Garthweb, or girthweb as it is sometimes termed, was the woven material from which horses' saddle girths were made and appears to have featured in a thriving cottage industry. According to the inventories attached to some local wills it is evident that the requisite materials for this trade were grown locally i.e. flax and hemp. Both required good fertile soil and Sale situated in the ancient flood plain of the River Mersey possessed rich alluvial soil and a high water table. The spun fibres of the flax and hemp could be used to make linen while the coarse more hard wearing woven hemp could be used for coarse clothes, sacks and the garthweb.

But Sale and Ashton-upon-Mersey could not remain immune from the scientific and political developments affecting the rest of the country. The Industrial Revolution made its impact in 1765 in the form of the Duke of Bridgewater's Canal which provided another

means of transportation for both goods and people. It may also have helped the growth of Sale, though the credit for that mainly belonged to the railway in the nineteenth century, and it is that century which saw the locality grow from a rural district with a population of 1,597 in 1801, to the beginnings of an urban area with a population of 11,241 in 1891.

National events too affected the community in the early years of the nineteenth century. The Napoleonic threat had been growing and fears that a French invasion was imminent led to the formation of

The uniform belonging to Capt. John Moore of the Ashton-upon-Mersey cum Sale Volunteers.

many local militia or the equivalent of the second World War Home Guard, which were to be used to repel any invading armies. Accordingly a local force was mustered in about 1803 and under the captaincy of a local man called John Moore formed the Ashton-upon-Mersey cum Sale Volunteers. During their existence they carried out manoeuvres on Sale Moor and on one occasion assisted in a review of 6,000 Volunteers from surrounding areas, though the local group itself numbered only about 80 to 100 men.

The Enclosure of Sale

This period too witnessed disturbing events at home for the ordinary villager. In 1805 an Act of Parliament was passed to enclose 'a certain Common called Sale Moor, and other Waste Lands, containing in the Whole One Hundred and fifty-two acres'. This was part of the nationwide movement of the process of enclosure which was gradually changing the English landscape of open fields farmed by all the villagers, into a landscape cut up into separate fields bounded by hedges or walls. In the open-field system there were generally two or three so-called fields farmed by all the villagers including the Lord of the Manor; the so-called fields being divided into long strips of land allocated to each person and being divided from each other by open drains and plough furrows. In addition to these, the surrounding rough grazing lands and woods would be shared communally i.e. they all had common rights, and it was these common lands that often caused controversy. By the nineteenth century enclosures, the movement had been going on for several centuries with the result that many people were losing their rights on the Common to cut turf, gather fuel, pasture an animal etc. Even if a peasant made a successful claim to the ownership of a piece of land, the cost of hedging it could be so prohibitive that he was often forced to sell it and the result was he suddenly had no livelihood and nowhere to grow his own food. The only people whose rights were assured under law, were the Lord of the Manor and the Incumbent of the Parish. Hence many folk were either thrown onto the charity of the parish or migrated to the towns where the products of the Industrial Revolution provided employment for some. In the township of Sale there seems to be some evidence to support a theory that some of the land was enclosed in the early seventeenth century, though the main enclosure documentation refers to the Act of 1805. But even in as small an area as Sale it is evident that the result of enclosure for some people was poverty, and subsequent Sale Township minutes began to mention poor relief measures for the first time.

Spies and Strangers

Times were therefore far from easy; abroad Napoleon continued to provide a threat which he extended into economic sanctions against England which in turn caused devastation to trade here. Goods piled up in the major warehouses in large towns such as Manchester; the price of wheat escalated and unemployment rose. Parallel to this the textile market was being affected by unscrupulous manufacturers producing inferior goods by using the broad frame worked by semi-skilled or female labour instead of making higher quality goods produced on the narrow frame manned by skilled labour. As a response to

the poverty caused by these events the 'Luddites' resorted to the destruction of isolated weaving frames in cottages as well as those in the larger mills in many northern and midland towns. In such an atmosphere of general unrest the Sale Township meeting, the forerunner of today's system of local government, issued a warning to its local residents in April 1812.

"That this meeting does particularly recommend it to the Publicans in the Neighbourhood to allow no improper tippling in their Houses but to shut them up at 10 o'clock in the Evening to discourage all Conversation tending to inflame the Public Mind, and as it is suspected that evil disposed Persons are travelling about the Country to excite a Spirit of Discontent and Uneasiness, they are requested to be particularly watchful of all strangers who may enter their Houses."

At the same meeting their remarks on the local poor folk seem symptomatic of the age:–

"That this Meeting feels for the present Suffering of the Poor and wishing to afford them all proper Relief does most highly disapprove of asking Charity by going from House to House in Numbers, and that all Persons doing so or using any Expressions tending to inflame or make uneasy the Minds of their Neighbours will be excluded from any Benefit of the above Subscription (for the relief of the poor) in the Distribution of which regard will be had to the Character of the Applicants."

The Railway Age

However, time went by and the economic situation improved somewhat but the 1840's witnessed an event in Sale which irrevocably started the pattern of change. In 1849 the Manchester South Junction and Altrincham Railway was opened. Remembering that a few

ANNO QUADRAGESIMO QUINTO

GEORGII III. REGIS.

****

Cap. 20.

An Act for inclosing Lands in the Township of *Sale*, in the Parish of *Ashton-upon-Mersey*, in the County Palatine of *Chester*.   [5th *April* 1805.]

WHEREAS there are within the Township of *Sale*, in the Parish of *Ashton-upon-Mersey*, in the County Palatine of *Chester*, a certain Common called *Sale Moor*, and other Waste Lands, containing in the Whole One hundred and fifty-two Acres or thereabouts, after the Rate of Eight Yards to the Rod or Perch (commonly called *Cheshire* Measure,: And whereas *William Egerton* Esquire, and *George John Legh* Esquire, claim to be Owners of the Soil of the said Common and Waste Lands : And whereas *Richard Popplewell Johnson* Clerk, is Patron and Rector of the Rectory, Parish, and Parish Church of *Ashton-upon-Mersey* aforesaid, of which the said Township of *Sale* is Parcel, and as such is entitled to the Tythes yearly arising and growing due within the said Township of *Sale* : And whereas the said *William Egerton, George John Legh*, the Right Honourable *George Harry* Earl of *Stamford* and *Warrington, Charles White, Lawrence Wright, Joseph Atkinson, George Ashton, John Moore, William Whitelegg, Henry Baxter, Peter Heward*, and several other Persons, are Owners and Proprietors of divers Lands,

[*Loc. & Per.*]   5 A   Tenements,

miles down the road was the burgeoning Cottonopolis of Manchester, and Sale was a pleasant rural district on its outskirts, now equipped with good access routes, it is not surprising that the growth of both areas became inter-related. Sale suddenly became a desirable area in which to build one's residence, away from the pressures of the city but within easy reach by train. Thus the rising middle class of merchants settled in Sale and also Altrincham and subsequently transformed them into the urban communities shown by some of the following photographs.

As a result of this increase in population and the added stimulus this created for local traders, consequently giving rise to a more complex community, local government was faced with an increasing need for better facilities. This was not just a local problem though, for the 1840's saw a growing national movement towards the realization that many problems of society stemmed from inadequate sanitation in many of the recently enlarged communities. As a result a series of Public Health Acts was passed giving ratepayers the right to petition for the establishment of Local Boards of Health to deal with water supplies, drainage, road maintenance, refuse and the like and to appoint medical officers of health. Sale eventually became a Board of Health in 1867 though the local Township meetings had been taking some measures to alleviate these problems prior to this date. In 1866 for instance one of the last major outbreaks of cholera occurred in Britain and in Sale the township was warned that it should take every precaution to stem any outbreak by establishing a Vigilance Committee whose duty it would be to make a house to house visitation and ensure every precaution was

taken to stop any epidemics. Accordingly the duties were handed to the already existing Nuisances Committee which dealt with any unpleasant jobs in the community. By the 1880's Sale had its first Medical Officer of Health who regularly reported on the state of the district; reports which sometimes belie the seemingly idyllic settings shown in the early photographs. In June 1883 he noted that:–
"During the warm moist weather there have been many and grievous complaints of smells arising from the sewer ventilators. Apropos of these I would with permission of the chair bring before your notice an arrangement for producing a more thorough ventilation."

By the end of 1895 the situation had improved slightly but it still did not meet the standards required by the Medical Officer of Health who reported 14 cases of diptheria and 6 cases of typhoid fever while noting in his

conclusion that:–
"Though, from time to time we have had complaints of nuisance arising from the sewer ventilations, on the whole there have been fewer than usual. There is, however room for improvement in this respect, as also in the state of some of our roads with regard to dust. This summer the Chester Road was barely adequately watered."

But amidst all these problems there was a lighter side to life shown in the number of social organisations established during the later part of the nineteenth century. One of these groups was the Minnehaha Amateur Minstrels who first saw the gas-light in April 1877 in an effort to raise money for Sale Cricket Club, and at a later date they were involved in other local charitable concerns. In a history they wrote of their own troupe the first members are depicted in oval Victorian

Extracts from The Minnehaha Amateur Minstrels, edited by Nelson Rusden, c 1896.

photographs with many wearing stiff wing collars and invariably sporting magnificent moustaches, but the ensuing pages show these seemingly sedate gentlemen in every possible minstrel guise.

Reorganisation

As the century drew to a close there were further developments in the structure of local government which in turn affected Sale. The 1894 Local Government Act replaced the old Boards of Health and established urban and rural district councils, and in turn gave them a wider range of duties, though in some areas they were subordinate to the county councils. Thus Sale became Sale Urban District Council in 1894, though some aspects of administration, for instance education, came under the general authority of the Cheshire County Council. Ashton-upon-Mersey became an urban district in 1895 but eventually amalgamated with Sale in 1930.

With the coming of the twentieth century both areas, while expanding greatly in terms of population and housing, still harboured many places of good market gardening and farming land. But with the growth of the community and the increased awareness of the need for better local facilities in the nation as a whole, came the creation of the Fire Service, the various welfare authorities and all the other services now normally associated with local government. By the 1930's Sale and Ashton-upon-Mersey had grown to such an extent that they were eligible to become a borough, receiving their Charter of Incorporation in 1935 and becoming jointly recognised as the Sale Borough Council.

At this point in its history the Borough still

Sale Old Hall was used as a hospital for Belgian casualties during the First World War.

possessed many areas of open land but it can be argued that the Second World War was responsible for finally removing the vestiges of the old agricultural way of life from the few remaining tracts of farmland. The results of the blitz on Manchester necessitated much slum clearance which, combined with the fact that much of the city housing had outlived its useful lifespan, made it essential to find new housing land. Consequently neighbouring districts had to assist with the housing problem which had in turn been exacerbated by the post war population rise, and in Sale this meant that much of the old agricultural land on the Ashton-upon-Mersey side of Washway Road was used for the building of large council house estates. These were variously termed the Manchester Overspill Estate, the Racecourse Estate etc.

At the time of writing Sale and Ashton-upon-Mersey are of course no longer predominantly agricultural communities.

Many of the large old detached properties made originally for the merchants of Manchester have either been converted into flats or demolished to make way for smaller housing units. Shopping facilities have also changed radically from the School Lane of the 1860's which contained the occasional market garden, to the School Road of the 1960's when a shopping precinct was extended from one side of the road. This emphasis on change continued in the north of the Borough as well, where the ten years from 1970 saw the development of a motorway and the recreational area of Sale Water Park. Finally in 1974 the community was subjected to the major upheaval of Local Government reorganisation when the old Sale Borough Council was amalgamated with the neighbouring districts of Altrincham, Stretford and Urmston to form the administrative unit of Trafford Metropolitan Borough.

Rose Cottage, School Road

This gives one an idea of how rural Sale must have seemed before it made the nineteenth century transition from a village community into an urban development area. Even the designation of this highway shows the changes during this period. In the early part of the nineteenth century it was called School Lane but somewhere during the period 1845–1876 it changed to become known as School Road.

The sight of the couple tending their small market garden might have been repeated throughout Sale innumerable times, as the 1876 Ordnance Survey map shows a preponderance of greenhouses and small holdings throughout the area; an activity obviously helped by the fertile soil, in part due to the alluvium washed down by the River Mersey over the centuries, and a relatively high water table.

School Road 1877

A view taken looking up School Road from its junction with Washway Road. On the left is the Old Bull's Head Inn, the precursor of the present Victorian building. Further along past the white buildings was a small cottage used as a smithy, this later became the site of Woolworths store and later still 'Shoppers World'. On the other side of the road there are numerous posters one of which advertises a forthcoming meeting of local ratepayers.

School Road around 1877

This photograph looks down the road towards Washway Road at the right-hand side beyond the delivery vehicle. At the time of writing the majority of the property shown here still exists though the shop frontages have been radically altered. Beginning at the left the shops included an ironmonger's premises, a fishmonger's belonging to Mr. Thomas Dodd and a watchmaker and silversmith by the name of Mr. Thomas Barlow. Further down the road was a house and garden bordering on Hayfield Street, both of which were demolished to enable the road to be widened. At No. 77 was Robinson's butcher's shop. In common with several other butchers in the area he grazed his sheep and cattle locally and slaughtered them in his own locally licensed slaughterhouse. Even by the turn of the nineteenth century there were still facilities for grazing stock in Sale, e.g. Gill the butcher on Sale Station Bridge possessed fields opposite Sale Library and more where Springfield School now stands.

Sale Market

Over the years the growing community found it necessary to set up a market shown here at Christmas time 1910. It was regularly situated on a plot of land at the right-hand side of Sale Town Hall before that building was extended towards Chapel Road. Eventually an entirely new Town Hall was built on the present site in 1914 compelling the market to seek fresh space opposite the Vine Inn on Washway Road. It remained on this land for only a few years before this area too was required for building purposes, and in the latter part of the 1920's it moved to a covered site next to the Waggon & Horses public house on Cross Street before finally closing down a few years later.

Depite the large bunch of bananas in the forefront of the photograph, the old market at the side of the Town Hall must have mirrored the market gardening community of which it was part. Some of the root vegetables, salad crops and flowers would have been derived from local market gardens, though live poultry and rabbits and some items of clothing were also available.

The Old Town Hall

Before 1875 the Sale Local Board held its meetings in temporary offices in a house in School Lane (Road) later moving to premises at the back of the Township School. By this date the business of local government was expanding and it was decided to purchase a building solely for use as Council Offices. In 1875, the same year as street lighting was first introduced into Sale, a residence called 'Oaklands' at No. 4 School Road was purchased and became the forerunner of the present Town Hall. Illustrated here, these early Council offices were situated on part of the land now occupied by the present Town Hall and Library.

By 1914 the work of the Sale Urban District Council had outgrown the converted gentleman's residence which was consequently demolished to provide space for a new Town Hall. The foundation stone of this building was laid in May 1914 by Mr. James McDonald, Chairman of the Public Offices Committee; though extensions were commenced in 1937. By July 1940 these additions to the original 1914 building were complete and were formally opened by the Mayor, Alderman G. F. Gordon, but by

that time the country was involved in the turmoil of the Second World War. This dealt a severe blow to the new building which was set on fire by a German incendiary bomb in December 1940. Part of the resultant damage can be seen here in a photograph taken about 1949; the rebuilding not being completed until 1952, nearly twelve years after the bombing.

Broad Road

The Old Smithies

This was one of a number of blacksmiths' premises in Sale and Ashton-on-Mersey during the nineteenth century. Shown here in about 1900, in the form of the low building at the left-hand side of the photograph, it stood on Broad Road just before the junction with Old Hall Road.

In the distance one can see a light coloured horse drawn carriage; this was the old horse bus which was painted yellow and which ran people to and from the Old Smithy and Sale Railway Station. In front of the old bus and heading towards the camera is one of the local grocer's delivery vans. Both these vehicles would have provided work for the nearby blacksmiths in an age

when there would be numerous horses in the community, ranging from those used for private means of transport in the wealthier households to those used for pulling milk, grocery and coal delivery vehicles. In market gardening and farming communities such as those of Sale and Ashton-on-Mersey there would also be much farm work, the horses that pulled the plough would need to be shod, occasionally the ploughshare itself would need repairing, and wooden wheels constructed by the wheelwright would require the blacksmith's skills in providing the finishing iron band that went round the circumference. Finally some of the more prosperous households would patronize local blacksmiths for the production of wrought iron fencing and gates.

Broad Road

Northenden Road about 1900

A typical weekday scene in the days when many Sale roads were still cobbled and before Manchester trams ran along this route. This view was taken looking up Northenden Road towards the Legh Arms Hotel in the distance; on the right is Warrener Street and on the left Temple Road.

At the right-hand side of the picture at 132 Northenden Road was Marsh's grocery shop seen here advertising the then popular 'Mazawatte' tea, 'Thomas' soaps and Bovril. Next door there lived Miss Mary Ann Marsh, a draper and next door to her was the fruiterer Mr. Robert Jones. Further along there were several butchers evident here by the carcasses hanging outside the shops; also bootmakers and painters shops. On the left-hand side at the corner of Temple Road was the fruit and beer retailing establishment of Mr. Jeremiah J. Wilkinson, now the site of the Temple Inn, and next door to him was a confectionery shop run by Mr. Walter G. Foden.

Passing all these premises and featuring somewhere in the lives of most people at the time was the rhythmical sound of the horse and cart delivering goods to all parts of the village and seen here in what must have been a busy thoroughfare even at the end of the nineteenth century.

John Wood's Store, Northenden Road

The grocery and general store trading under the name of John Wood was one of the largest businesses in the district and can be seen pictured here in a photograph taken in 1903. The property was situated at 170 Northenden Road near the junction with Marsland Road and started life as a smithy and blacksmith's forge plus two cottages in the 1850's, and was extended in the 1870's to take the form shown here.

Originally Mr. & Mrs. Thomas Wilkinson established the shop in 1856 but Mr. Wilkinson died in a tragic accident while still comparatively young. His widow Ann later remarried a Mr. John Wood of Wallbank Farm, Sale and it is his name which can be seen above the door. However, the guiding force behind the business was always his wife, now Mrs. Ann Wood. The premises comprised a grocery store, a post office, and a wine and spirit department, but they also sold bread which they baked themselves in a bakehouse situated in a building just off the photograph at the left-hand side. Part of their delivery service can be seen here in the form of the horse-drawn van, though the business retained several horses which they stabled at the back of the property. Eventually the business acumen of Mrs. Ann Wood extended this service to supply groceries to surrounding areas as far as Chorlton and Baguley.

Advertisements around the shop displayed the well known brands of the day including Highland Whisky, Spratt's Patent Dog Cakes, Hartley's Marmalade and Colman's Mustard and Starch. At the right-hand side of the building just beneath the eaves can be seen a hoist for moving bags of grain and other produce in and out of the property.

In 1905 Mrs. Ann Wood died causing a great loss to many people in the district and on the Manchester Grocer's Exchange, and in 1912 the business was sold to Wilson's Brewery who continued to run it as a grocery.

Ashton Lane

At the end of the nineteenth century there were many rows of small shops in the locality. One of these areas, now demolished, is shown here along Ashton Lane near its junction with Washway Road and Cross Street in about 1900. On the corner at the right-hand side was a grocery store kept by Mr. John Clarke while other shops in the row included a drapery shop kept by Mrs. Martha Pendlebury, an upholsterer's run by Mr. Frederick Murphy, the brush dealer Mr. Edward Price, the establishment of the dressmakers Misses Jane and Alice Fox, another grocery shop operated by Mr. Henry Deane and a confectionery business run by Mrs. M. Freeman.

Cross Street

The inset photograph of the 1920's showing the No. 49 tramcar in the vicinity of the River Mersey, clearly shows the problems created by that river. For centuries it had periodically burst its banks and flooded the surrounding district making passage across this area often hazardous. In 1750 it was noted that in winter and frequently summer the flooding made the river impassable being responsible for loss of life and delaying the post, as Cross Street was part of the post road from London to Manchester. It was not until well into the twentieth century when the old No. 49 tramcar had been replaced by the No. 112 bus service, that man really brought this section of the River Mersey under control.

Over the years there have been various suggestions that the name Cross Street should be removed from this section of the A56 in preference to the name Chester Road. Fortunately opinion has always been on the side of the retention of Cross Street because of its historic origins. It was probably so named because crosses were invariably put at the places where rivers were crossed enabling people to know which track to take in going through the water.

The other picture of Cross Street was taken at the junction with Chapel Road about the year 1900. At this period Cross Street was a bustling shopping area containing all manner of traders. Just off the photograph at the left-hand side where one can catch a glimpse of railing, was the entrance to the Volunteer Public House. Next door, where the gentleman in a white apron is standing, was the saddler's shop run by Mr. Henry Penney. His neighbours were Miss Charlotte Moore, the dressmaker and William Hampson and Sons, grocers. In this row of shops the jovial Mr. Thomas Wallis had his tripe shop and every evening he could be seen round the district selling his hot peas and trotters which he kept warm by means of a small lamp. Further along, near the Mersey Road corner just before the sign advertising the shop belonging to M. E. Howe, was the Coffee Tavern run by Mr. Frederick Vickers. Between the years 1889 and 1909 he was host not only to local people such as farmers returning from the Manchester markets, but also to thousands of men and women who were devotees of the new craze of cycling; with many of the Manchester cycling clubs stopping in his establishment for refreshment. Here he provided all manner of meals from breakfast to tea and advertised steaks at any hour of the day. He also had a dance room and stabling facilities and was locally known as the man who would help you out if you had a spot of trouble.

Crossing the road past all the tradesmen's delivery vehicles was the butcher's shop run by Mr. John Bailey at the corner of Chapel Road and Cross Street, his neighbouring businessmen being greengrocers, confectioners and the stationer Mr. Jesse Croft. On the corner of King Street, beneath the advertisement for Colman's Starch was yet another grocery shop belonging to Mr. Arthur Whitrod.

Washway Road

Wovenden's Chemist's Shop, Sale Road

At the top of School Road, opposite the present Sale Town Hall, Henry Wovenden had his chemist's shop. Here he offered his renowned 'Universal Cough Mixture' and sold mineral and aerated waters which he prepared in his works in Springfield Road. According to various people writing notes on their memories of Sale around 1900, Henry Wovenden was a well loved local personality and is accredited with having his own singular sense of humour. Apparently anyone asking him for a tip would be given a box of Beecham's pills and assured that if they weren't successful they could always have another box!

He continued to actively participate in the business until he was 82 in the year 1924, when he finally retired and in the following year celebrated his diamond jubilee wedding anniversary.

Washway Road

These shops are at the beginning of Washway Road; School Road is just off the picture towards the left-hand side. The view was taken in the late 1870's and although the facades of the buildings have been altered the properties are still used by various local businesses.

The main business shown here belonged to the Birkenhead family who ran a thriving florists, nursery shop and general garden store at No. 19 where the conservatory it situated, and a Post Office and general stationers next door at No. 17. This was the age when many Victorian gardeners and owners of large estates showed a passionate interest in the culture of ferns. Fern walks and fern houses were established and other specimens brought into the house by means of the Wardian case. Birkenhead's in Sale supplied this market by creating such an excellently stocked fern nursery that "The Gardeners Chronicle" reviewing such businesses wrote, "Of these nursery establishments none is better known . . . than that of Messrs. W. & J. Birkenhead of Sale, near Manchester".

In the Post Office section they also sold postcards of contemporary local views, many of which are now collectors' items. Some years after this photograph was taken the front of No. 17 was modernized to include an ornamental section of masonry near the roof; this contained a sign for the Post Office which, while no longer used, can still partially be seen today.

Moving towards the left-hand side other shops in the row included a baby linen establishment, and the confectionery shop belonging to Miss Alice Forshaw at No. 11 where a rudimentary form of blind covers the window.

Woodheys Grange

The Avenue

It was constructed about 1860 for the local landowner
Mr Samuel Brooks. At this date it was known as Brooks's
Avenue and was the site of a handful of elegant detached
houses of which Woodheys Grange was an example. In
1877 when this photograph was taken, the Washway
Road entrance to The Avenue was protected by an
imposing wall and gates. 'The Lodge' shown here is still
recognisable today, although it no longer has a small
spire.

Sale Township School

Education

The growth of population in Sale during the nineteenth century led to a need for larger school accommodation at a time when this expenditure was not borne out of the rates. It was not until 1902 that elementary education became financed by the local rates and Sale was called upon to form a School Board; the last school board in England. Prior to this education had been provided by voluntary schools associated with various churches and also a body of Trustees.

The Trust can be traced back to the days when School Lane, later School Road, had taken its name from the Township School at the top of the road. Illustrated here in the late 1870's it had been built in 1800 to replace two cottages used as a school in Springfield Road. The old school shown here was a result of a public subscription to which the Duke of Bridgewater made a substantial contribution. The building was situated about half way between the present National Westminster Bank near the Sale Town Hall, and Boots the chemist at the entrance to the shopping precinct. It provided teaching facilities for about 150 children and also accommodation for the school master. One curious claim associated with this school was its supposed brief link with the notorious 'cat burglar' Charlie Peace. Various old pupils writing in the early part of the twentieth century mention Charlie Peace as having once given violin lessons or a lantern slide show in the school. Peace, incidentally, was hanged in 1879 for killing a policeman who tried to apprehend him while in the act of housebreaking in a Manchester suburb.

Eventually the old Sale Township School no longer met the requirements of the community and in 1879 an even larger school was built in School Road, but even this became insufficient for the needs of the expanding population. So after much planning a new building was opened in 1907 and became known as the Springfield Council School. The opening ceremony is depicted in the three photographs, showing people arriving outside the school in Springfield Road and collecting together in the playground. By now the Cheshire County Council had assumed responsibility for the school though it was placed under the local auspices of the Sale and Ashton Administrative Sub-Committee for Education. Mr. John Morley, of Sale was Chairman of this committee and was present at the ceremony together with Mr. T. F. Wainwright, the Chairman of the Springfield School Managers, who officially opened the building. In the other two photographs Mr. John Morley is the gentleman with the white beard and a flower in his buttonhole. Pictured with the large group of people he can be seen accepting a gold key on behalf of the school's architect, and in the other photograph, where he is wearing a top hat, he can be seen chatting to the headmaster of the Senior Department, Mr. Adam Watson, the gentleman wearing a bowler hat.

The opening of Springfield Road School 1907.

SALE & ASHTON-ON-MERSEY TECHNICAL SCHOOL.

SYLLABUS OF THE COOKERY CLASSES,

And particulars respecting other Classes in Domestic Subjects,

FOR THE

1897-98 SESSION, SECOND TERM,

COMMENCING ✤ MONDAY, ✤ JANUARY ✤ 10, ✤ 1898.

Cookery Classes, held at the Public Library, Sale.

Teacher - Miss E. C. FOTHERGILL.

On Monday and Thursday Afternoons, 3 to 5; Monday and Thursday Evenings, 7 to 9.

Programme for Afternoons.	Programme for Evenings.
1. Chestnut Soup, Baked Turbot, Banville Cream, Imperial Cakes.	1. Irish Stew, Shrewsbury Pudding, Victoria Cakes.
2. Scallops of Veal, Pear Charlotte, Chocolate Biscuits.	2. Fried Plaice, Ground Rice Pudding, Swiss Roll.
3. Chicken Fricassee, Walnut Baskets, Ham Savouries.	3. Bread and Buns.
4. Rabbit Soup, Curried Eggs, Apples à la Moville.	4. Lentil Soup, Madeira Cheese Cakes, Oatmeal Biscuits.
5. Cod with Shrimps, Alexandra Pudding, Breakfast Rolls.	5. Steak and Kidney Pudding, Brussels Sprouts, Fat Rascals.
6. Beefsteak and Mushroom Pudding, Cream Fritters, Simnel Cake.	6. Baked Cod, Parsley Sauce, Chocolate Blanc Mange, Simnel Cake.
7. Fried Sole, Chocolate Pudding, Chelsea Buns.	7. Meat Pies, Merton Pudding, Almond Drops
8. Russian Pasties, Sweet Jelly, Marlborough Cake.	8. Beef Tea, Fricasseed Eggs, Luncheon Cake.
9. Sole à la Bohémienne, Potato Patties, Apricot Soufflé.	9. Chops with Vegetables, Invalid's Pudding, Lemon Sandwiches.
10. Noisettes of Mutton, Velvet Cream, Sweet Cigarettes, Vienna Bread.	10. Sausage Popovers, Apple Gateau, Omelet Soufflé.
11. Beef Olives, Meringue Tarts, Marbled Cake, Cheese Straws.	11. Bachelor's Stew, College Pudding, Jubilee Biscuits.
12. White Sombise Soup, West Riding Pudding, Almond Cuts.	12. Fish Cutlets, Valencia Cornets, Hot Cross Buns.
Subject to Alteration.	Subject to Alteration.

Laundry Class held on Friday Evenings from 7 to 9.

Teacher - Miss FLORENCE OWEN.

Dressmaking Classes:—Teacher - - Miss L. TEMPEST.

TECHNICAL SCHOOL	MONDAY AFTERNOON	3 to 5.
	MONDAY EVENING	7 to 9.
	THURSDAY AFTERNOON	3 to 5.
	THURSDAY EVENING	7 to 9.

MILLINERY CLASSES.

... School on Tuesday afternoons, from

The Free Library and Technical School

The building shown here was the first purpose built public library in Sale and was the result of a bequest by Mr. John Brooks, M.P. for the Altrincham Division of Cheshire, who bequeathed £100 to be devoted to the best interests of the poor in Sale. As a result, those responsible for administering the directions of the will decided to use the money as a nucleus of a Public Free Library in the hope that eventually the local authority would adopt the Public Libraries Act and maintain such a facility out of the rates. The first step in the scheme was taken by the trustees of the old Township School who formed themselves into a committee to put the bequest into effect and in 1887 a free library was opened in a room of the Township School in School Road. In 1890 a meeting of Sale ratepayers adopted a resolution to implement the Public Libraries Acts of 1855 and 1889 and accordingly a subscribers committee was formed, a public subscription held, and in a matter of a year enough money was raised to be able to erect the library shown here. It was formally opened on 7th March 1891 and handed over to the local authority who would now maintain it out of the rates, though at that time the amount of rates that could be spent on libraries was strictly limited by the Public Libraries Act to an amount not exceeding a rate of 1d in the £, except for a few very large towns.

The first building lasted until 1936 when the books and staff moved to temporary premises in the Technical School next door and the old library was demolished and a new building (the present library) opened in 1938.

The Free Library and Technical School stood at the junction of Tatton Road and Tatton Place, Sale in the early years of the 1900's. The library on the right-hand side was in roughly the same position as the present building, though the Technical School on the left-hand side still exists in the form of the Town Hall Annexe.

Evening or continuation classes started in Sale in 1895 but were scattered throughout the district in an attempt to make education more widely available. Whilst initially attracting nearly 500 people in the first year, the attendance decreased and there were complaints that art and science were not adequately covered. Accordingly, the new Technical School shown here was opened in March 1897 in an effort to provide better facilities all under one roof, though a few classes were still held in other buildings. Not only did it aim to provide for Sale residents, but also those in Ashon-upon-Mersey, as by now both townships had joined together for the matter of technical instruction, though it was some years before the two authorities amalgamated for all aspects of local government.

Sir William Cunliffe Brooks, M.P. for the Altrincham Division of Cheshire, opened the new Sale and Ashton-upon-Mersey Technical School amidst a parade by the local Fire Brigade, displays of flags and streamers in Tatton Road and an exhibition of arts and crafts arranged in commemoration of the occasion. The architect, Mr. A. G. McBeath, the surveyor of the Sale Urban District Council, commented on the opening day that he had designed the building to harmonize with the public library with which it was now connected by means of a corridor on the first floor. On the outside of the school, over each door was an ornamental niche, constructed out of Ruabon terra cotta and designed to hold two figures illustrating Science and Art. These niches are still visible today, though they do not contain any statues.

Inside the school there were two classrooms in the basement, two on the ground floor and one large classroom for the use of the art department on the first floor. This connected with the upstairs library lecture hall by means of a corridor shown in the centre of the photograph thus facilitating movement between both buildings. In fact not only was the Technical School used for classes but also the library lecture hall, though the latter was also used for recreational lectures as well.

The Fire Brigade

In 1914 the Sale & Ashton-on-Mersey Fire Brigade purchased their first motorised 'Dennis' Fire Engine seen here in front of the old Fire Station doors at the back of the present Town Hall. This building no longer houses the Fire Station though it is used for garaging Council vehicles. Technically this motor vehicle was known as the 'Dennis' 60 B.H.P. 400/450 gallon turbine motor fire engine and escape carrier and first aid machine. It had solid rubber tyres and was painted in red with white lines and gold leaf mouldings and had a 40 ft. escape, and a first aid tank with a capacity of 30 to 40 gallons positioned behind the driver's seat. Two men could sit in the front, another two could be accommodated on the back step and if need be four men could be placed either side, hence the brass hand rails which can be seen between the two seated firemen. The large mounted bell was so positioned near the steering wheel that it could be continuously rung by a fireman holding on to the side of the vehicle. In all, the new fire engine cost £990.

The gentleman pictured to the far right of the photograph was the Superintendent Mr. J. Royle, some of his men included Mr. C. Steains and Mr. G. Jones positioned left and right on the top row and Mr. G. Alcock, second from the right on the bottom row.

All these photographs depict various stages in the history of the Sale Fire Brigade which was formed in 1872 when a hose cart and various fire appliances were purchased. Towards the end of the nineteenth century their equipment included a horse drawn fire escape as shown in both the early pictures. These views were taken at the side of the old Council Offices and Fire Station which were then located in a house on the site of the present Town Hall. In the photograph showing four firemen one can see School Road in the distance behind the trees. It is interesting to note that at this period the firemen were wearing solid brass helmets, but as the years went by and electricity was introduced into most districts these were discontinued in the interest of safety, as brass would conduct a current of electricity in fires involving electric cables. In the other early photograph showing seven firemen, the gentleman at the far right-hand side was Chief Officer Hunt who was unfortunately killed in a fire at Brooklands Hotel, Sale.

During 1898 the Sale and Ashton districts combined their fire protection services to form the Sale and Ashton-on-Mersey Joint Fire Brigade, a year which also saw the decision to purchase a steam fire engine (Right).

At this date the equipment was still pulled by horses, though the local newspaper reported in May 1914

that excellent speed records could still be achieved and quoted an example of a recent fire where a call had been received from Northenden well over three miles away and the Fire Brigade had attended the blaze within twenty minutes. This involved someone running up the stairs to the top of the Town Hall and ringing the fire bell to signal the voluntary firemen, who with one exception lived off the premises. Horses had then to be brought from the nearby cab stand at Sale Station, being borrowed for the occasion by prior arrangement, rather than belonging to the Fire Brigade. Having harnessed the horses, assembled both equipment and men they would then thunder along the road to the accompaniment of the shrill noise of the hand bell.

Men at Work

The inset photograph shows a gang of men employed repairing the small paving stones or setts in Northenden Road at the beginning of the twentieth century. Small granite or sandstone blocks or setts about 3½ to 4½ inches deep were in common use as road building material during the nineteenth century, though by the date of the photograph many roads were made of water bound macadam. However, with the growth of motor traffic this type of surface rapidly disintegrated giving rise to a 'dust' problem which was eventually eliminated by occasionally spraying the road surface with tar.

The large wooden mallets these men are holding were known as paviour's mauls and were used for hammering the setts to the correct level. They were working on the area known as the cabmen's shelter where the old horse drawn cabs used to wait near the junction of Clarendon Road and Northenden Road. During the 1920's the Sale Urban District Council decided to change the use of the site and erected an electricity sub-station on the land.

A similar scene shows men at work at the junction of Hope Road and Baxter Road about the year 1900. The machine they were using was popularly described as a 'Tar Boiler' though it could be used to heat and distribute tar, pitch or bitumen and being heavy would have been towed to the site by either a horse or some form of early tractor. Containers or barrels of tar would be loaded into the machine by means of a crane mounted on front of the boiler. Once in the machine the tar would be heated until it became fluid and then sprayed onto the road surface by means of a hand pump or drawn off through a valve. The heat required in this process was supplied by a coal or coke fire beneath the boiler, the smoke being discharged from the tall chimney seen here at the left of the apparatus.

As one of the men is holding a ladle and there appear to be a pile of setts in the background it seems probable that they were involved in sett paving whereby the blocks of granite or sandstone would be laid on a stone base and grouted with hot pitch or bitumen applied by means of the long handled ladle.

A side view of the library during the early part of the nineteenth century. Pictured here are the Sale & Ashton-on-Mersey Joint Fire Brigade during fire practice.

The junction of Hope Road and Baxter Road

St. Anne's Church, Ashton-upon-Mersey

Churches

As the years passed by the growing communities of Sale and Ashton-upon-Mersey required more churches of varying denominations but the first in the area was that of the church of St. Martin in Ashton-upon-Mersey. Initially it was built to serve Sale and Carrington as well as Ashton though over the centuries as the population grew other churches were established, for instance the parish of St. Anne in Sale, separated from the Ashton church in 1866.

History maintains that the first church of St. Martin built of wood and dating from 1304, lasted until a particularly fierce storm in 1703 when it was so badly damaged that it had to be replaced by a new building of Lymm stone and Peover timber as illustrated here in a picture taken sometime before 1874. This photograph bears only slight resemblance to the present day structure as Sir William Cunliffe Brooks, Member of Parliament for the Altrincham Division of Cheshire and son of the famous Manchester banker Samuel Brooks, erected the now familiar addition of a black and white clock tower in 1887 to commemorate Queen Victoria's Golden Jubilee.

Because of the age of the church it has been associated with several local legends, one of the most tragic occurring in the sixteenth century when it was said that the rector's daughter Sybil Tipping fell in love with the son of the De Trafford family who lived nearby. Her father had other ideas for his daughter and forbade any possible liaison with the De Trafford family with the result that one evening after he had followed them to their meeting place at a local mill, he overheard that they were planning to elope. Filled with vengeance he drew his sword and challenged the suitor during which the young man was killed. Distraught, Sybil was carried back home where she remained gravely ill for some time. As the weeks passed it became apparent that the tragic event had affected her sanity and rumour had it that from that time onwards she was virtually imprisoned in a room on the top floor of the rectory. All anyone ever heard of her again were the moans issuing from that room until one night she escaped and was never seen again. Legend maintains that the only trace she left was a track of footprints in the snow leading to her old trysting place at the mill and that on dark nights the ghost of a girl could be seen walking along this route.

Strangely enough years later when the old mill was being cleaned out it is said that the skeleton of a woman was discovered, whether it was that of Sybil is open to speculation.

The picture (left) shows the other side of church activity in Sale by illustrating the annual Procession of Witness held by St. Anne's Church in May 1914. After weeks of preparation the majority of local churches held an annual Whitsuntide procession with everyone being encouraged to join in both the walk round the neighbourhood and the treats and field day activities afterwards. At St. Anne's the walk was invariably held on Whit Friday when those in the parade would assemble outside the Sunday School between 1.30 p.m. and 2.00 p.m. The men from the St. Anne's Brotherhood would carry the main poles of the banner while the senior girls in the Bible class or higher Sunday School classes carried the main banner strings; the finer ribbons being allocated to some of the smaller girls. Most of the "banner girls" tried to dress alike and some carried shower bouquets, others small posies of flowers. Eventually the parade set off led by the church dignitaries and choir and including the people with the banner and the rest of the congregation. The route of the parade varied from year to year; one year it might cover Northenden Road to Poplar Grove and Marsland Road and the following year move from Northenden Road, Temple Road and Broad Road. During this period the procession would occasionally stop to sing a hymn and then move off and continue on its journey once more. In the days before World War II the event was one of the highlights of the year for many people and the procession attracted much interest from the inhabitants of Sale who would crowd the pavements to watch the parades. Other pre-war features were the picnic and sporting activities, invariably held at the end of the day either in a farm at Temple Road or a yard at the Brooklands Hotel. Here the adults could have a drink of tea while the children played games.

St. Martin's Church, Ashton-upon-Mersey

Sale Old Hall

When leaving the M63 for the Old Hall Road or walking along the Mersey Valley few people would perhaps associate the old dove cote, standing next to the motorway, with the remains of a building site that takes the history of Sale back to the thirteenth century. The area now in the vicinity of the Hardy Lane Extension, Rifle Road and the junction with the M63 once housed the building known as the Sale Old Hall.

It seems highly probable that the first Old Hall was the property of the locally influential Massey family who owned land in Sale in the early 1200's. Documentary evidence for the existence of the building is provided some centuries later in the Christopher Saxton map of 1577 which locates the site for the first time. It is also interesting to note that after the demolition of the hall, one of the date stones bearing the inscription '1600' was removed and fixed to the lodge at Worthington Park, though this date may have only been an approximation.

Perhaps an original thirteenth century property had fallen into a state of disrepair and had had to be demolished and rebuilt around the end of the sixteenth century, but unfortunately this is all supposition.

However, by about 1746, the Massey family having become extinct, the property passed in turn to the Nobles, the Mainwarings and later the Egertons of Tatton, finally coming into the possession of one John Moore. This was the same man who captained the Ashton-upon-Mersey cum Sale Loyal Volunteers at the beginning of the nineteenth century when Britain feared a Napoleonic invasion. In 1821 the Hall was tenanted by a Mrs. Bury who ran a school from the premises until they were purchased in 1838 by Mrs. M. Worthington. This lady was responsible for either demolishing or radically altering the property into the form shown in the photograph. Some years after the alterations in the year 1888 the property was rented by the locally famous Sir William Bailey who was renowned for both his scholastic attributes and engineering abilities. Originally Sir William's family had come from the Eccles and Salford area where his father had founded an engineering business which flourished under the management of the son. As an ardent Liberal he led an active life in local politics in Salford, becoming an Alderman in 1880 and in addition, in recognition of the work he had done in the enterprize of the opening of the Manchester Ship Canal, Queen Victoria conferred a knighthood upon him. The photographs show the interior of the Old Hall during the period of Sir William Bailey's residence, with the photograph of the library showing part of his famous collection of the works of Montaigne. The 'Togo' Pavilion in the garden is quite interesting in that it was constructed from materials which came from the great Manchester Royal Jubilee Exhibition which was held on a 32 acre site in Old Trafford in 1887 as a means of honouring Queen Victoria's Jubilee. In concept it was similar to the Great London Exhibition of 1851 in that it comprised a display of a vast array of products and skills from all over the Empire. Sir William, being Chairman of the Handicraft Section, no doubt took this opportunity to buy various items when the exhibition came to an end when large sections of the furniture and fittings were auctioned. The pavilion he built from some of the pieces was named after the Japanese Admiral Togo who led the Japanese fleet to victory in the Russo-Japanese war of 1905.

When Sir William Bailey vacated the Old Hall it ceased to be occupied by a single family and during World War I housed a number of Belgian refugees, and was shortly afterwards demolished. The story of the Hall does not end at this point as a quantity of the old bricks were re-used by local scouts in the 1920's in the building of the 1st Brooklands Scouts Headquarters in Eaton Road.

Today the Victorian dove cote situated near the Hardy Lane extension of the M63 is the last remnant of the Old Hall site. When the rest of the site was covered by the motorway the old dove cote was left near the new embankment and had to be partially filled with concrete in order to stabilise it.

The library

Inner hall

Trinity Methodist Church garden party at Sale Old Hall, c 1912. The gentleman sitting in the covered chair is Sir William Bailey

The corridor

The dining room

The Priory

At the beginning of this century there stood in Dane Road a house called 'The Priory'. It was occupied during the eighteenth century by the eminent Dr. Thomas White and later by his son Dr. Charles White.

Dr. Thomas White practised medicine in Manchester, eventually taking his son Dr. Charles White into an apprenticeship in the profession, where he became famous for his valuable work in the field of midwifery. The son also played a leading part in the foundation of the Public Infirmary in Manchester and was later responsible for the development of the hospital now known as St. Mary's.

Apart from his memorable work in obstetrics Dr. Charles White is also remembered for his association with the strange case of the 'Manchester Mummy'. One of his patients, a certain Miss Hannah Beswick, bequeathed him a large sum of money on condition that the doctor embalm her body after death and inspect it once a year. Apparently Miss Beswick's sister had experienced a narrow escape from being buried alive whilst in a trance and hence she wished to make herself secure from this fate by endeavouring to ensure that her body would be stored above ground and periodically inspected for one hundred years. The story goes that Dr. White complied with her wish and accordingly kept her mummified body in an old clock case on the roof of his country home, 'The Priory'. However, there is a certain amount of controversy over the sum supposedly bequeathed by Miss Beswick; some sources insist on a figure of £35,000, others of £20,000 whilst many believe that the figure was minimal. At any rate when Dr. White died in 1813 the mummified body passed into the hands of his friend Dr. Ollier who in turn left it to the Natural History Museum in Peter Street, Manchester, where it remained an object of curiosity until 1868 when the stipulated hundred years had expired and the museum was about to be dispersed. In that year it was finally interred at Harpurhey Cemetary.

On the death of Dr. Charles White the residence known as 'The Priory' entered into a period when it had numerous occupiers. Finally it became the property of A. H. Megson and after his death it was sold to the Sale Urban District Council in 1920 for £1,000, on condition that they allowed the building to remain in the same state for the next 20 years, but unfortunately they were not made responsible for repairs. Consequently by 1932 it had deteriorated so much that it had to be demolished.

Much confusion has arisen through the years over the name 'Priory'. In a pamphlet produced in 1921 reference is made to the building having been a monastery, later converted into a private residence. However, in recent years it has been proved that there is little or no evidence to support this theory as the house was built about 1711 and appears to have had no connection with a religious order. Had a previous religious building been erected on the site and a later private residence built on its place, is open to question. It has been suggested that the cellars were probably part of an old monastery but as they were constructed of brick this idea seems doubtful as well. Brick as a building material was not used in this area between the end of the Roman period and the Reformation.

Dr. Charles White

Church Lane

In the 1930's there still existed the occasional thatched cottage in the locality. This photograph shows the seventeenth or early eighteenth century thatched cottages in Church Lane, Ashton-on-Mersey immediately before their demolition in 1937.

They were once used as the residence of the curates of the Church of St. Martin, but latterly the properties fell into disrepair and came under the scrutiny of the local Sale Council who considered that they should be demolished as they were in such a delapidated state. Heated discussion both inside and outside the Council chamber followed but it was eventually agreed to demolish them. A representative of the Ancient Monuments Society visited the site but even he stated that there was very little of the original fabric left intact and therefore could not advise the restoration of the building.

Cross Street

Centuries ago there must have been many small thatched dwellings in Sale and Ashton but by 1930 they had become a rarity. These cottages stood on the east side of Cross Street between Hesketh Grove at the left-hand side of the cottages where the girl is standing, and Dargle Road at the right. Even at this date the property was becoming surrounded by the accoutrements of an increasingly technological society i.e. the street lighting and the tram rails in the road. But eventually the cottages themselves gave way to the new age and were demolished to widen the road and make way for the Department of Health and Social Security building.

Above: Miss Evelyn Hardy. Below: Mr James Whittaker the chauffeur.

Tyntesfield

In the early part of the nineteenth century the property now known as Tyntesfield was farmland until the locally famous banker Mr. Samuel Brooks bought the land in 1850 and erected the building. These pictures illustrate Tyntesfield in the 1920's when it was occupied by Mr. Fred Hardy who was born in 1860 as the second son of Mr. George Hardy of Hardy's Crown Brewery, Manchester. On the death of his father, Mr. Fred Hardy took over the brewing business, which he ran in conjunction with his brother Harry, and where he gained the reputation of being a shrewd businessman.

On his marriage to Miss Catherine Thompson of Timperley he made his home at Tyntesfield in the early 1880's, where he became known as a keen sportsman and ardent orchid enthusiast.

The rose garden

Mr N Hardy holding the horse with Fowler the groom

Probably Mr. Fred Hardy's proudest moment, when his horse
Happy Man won the Ascot Gold Cup in 1923. Happy Man
was both stabled at Tyntesfield and trained in the fields of
Ashton-upon-Mersey. Pictured here the results of both
Mr. Hardy's hobbies can be seen, his winning horse on one
hand and on the other one of his Odontoglossum type orchids
in his buttonhole.

The Bridgewater Canal

The most important factors in the development of Sale were the various advances in methods of transportation. The photograph here shows the section of the Bridgewater Canal on the side of Chapel Road leading to the approach to Sale Railway Station, in the 1870's. The Sale section of the Duke of Bridgewater's Canal was completed in 1765 and helped to facilitate the movement of fresh market garden produce from north Cheshire to the markets in Manchester, though it was constructed to enable the Duke to move coal from his mines at Worsley to Salford, Manchester and eventually Hollin Ferry, the Mersey river and Liverpool. At the right-hand side of the photograph several Bridgewater Colliery flat boats can be seen, each containing a quantity of coal which was also stored in this area. The small two-wheeled cart was also used for moving coal. Just past the coal wharf moving towards Stretford one can also see the crane and jib on the side of the canal where cargo could be loaded and unloaded.

    The 1759 Act of Parliament which enabled the canal to be cut and the Duke to transport his coal more economically by a method of cheap transport, opened up a route that eventually carried not only coal but fruit and vegetables and all manner of parcels and merchandise. A familiar scene in Sale would have been the sight of a slim barge gliding into view, pulled by a horse at full gallop and guided by a captain blowing a horn to announce their arrival. One such boat the 'Duchess Countess' made her daily journey from Warrington to Manchester for more than eighty years until the 1920's when the service

was finally discontinued. In the 1870's around the time this photograph was taken there were about 400 horses working on the canal enabling Sale residents to take the 'swift packet' to work in Manchester. The name for these boats was reflected locally in the name of the public house the Packet Inn, pictured on the left of the photograph as Chapel Road begins to swing away from the canal. Barges would regularly draw up here and the crew partake of refreshment before proceeding again.

    With today's mechanical aids it is often difficult to visualise the immense undertaking the cutting of this canal actually was to the people of the eighteenth century. A contemporary observation from a letter dated 1765 gives some idea of what an achievement this venture was by observing the construction of the canal in the vicinity of the Sale and Stretford boundary:–
"I found four hundred men at work, (though it was Sunday) in putting the finishing stroke to about two hundred yards of the canal, . . . with a number of loaded barges . . . One of these appeared like the hull of a collier, with its deck all covered after the manner of cabin, and having an iron chimney in the centre; this, on inquiry, proved to be the carpentry, but was shut up, being Sabbath day, as was another barge, which contained the smith's forge. Other vessels were loaded with soil, which was put into troughs, fastened together and rested on boards that lay across two barges; between each of these

was room enough to discharge the loading, by loosening some iron pins at the bottom of the troughs: other barges lay loaded with the foundation stones of the navigation canal or bridge, which is to hold the Duke's barges of coals and merchandise, intended to be carried across the Mersey. Near two thousand oak piles are already driven to strengthen the foundation of this Bridge. The carpenters on the Lancashire side were preparing the centre frame; and on the Cheshire, all hands, and may I say, all the water, at work in bringing down the soil, and beating the ground adjoining to the foundation of the bridge, which is designed to be covered with stone in a month, and finished in ten days more.

    I surveyed the Duke's men for two hours, and think that the industry of bees, or labour of ants, is not to be compared with them."

    The writer then goes on to mention that the engineer's men encountered more problems with the 'low and boggy' Sale meadows where:–
"At this place Mr. Brindley caused trenches to be made, and placed deal baulks in an erect position, backing and supporting them on the outside with other baulks laid in rows, and screwed fast together; and on the front side, he threw the earth and clay, in order to form his navigation canal. After thus finishing forty yards of his artificial river, he removed the baulks, and placed them again where the canal was designed to advance."

The Manchester South Junction and Altrincham Railway

Though the Bridgewater Canal undoubtedly helped put Sale on the map, the railway was responsible for transforming the rural village into an urban district. In 1845 an Act of Parliament was passed authorizing the construction of the Manchester South Junction and Altrincham Railway, though its passage through Parliament was not without problems for it would provide direct competition to the canal. Consequently Lord Francis Egerton, Chief Trustee of the Bridgewater Canal was eventually placated by an offer of £50,000 worth of shares in the railway and a guarantee of an 8% per annum return, as a result of which some of the canal land adjacent to the proposed railway track in Sale was offered to the railway company. Additionally the trustees offered to withdraw the competition of passenger boats from Timperley to Manchester once the line was opened, and finally the Manchester South Junction and Altrincham Railway Bill was given a smooth passage through Parliament.

The route was now clear for the operation to get underway, tenders were duly placed and the section of the line from Manchester to Altrincham was received by the contractor John Brogden, a Sale builder. After innumerable problems over land ownership and compulsory purchase orders the track was eventually extended to Altrincham and in May 1849 enough of the track was complete for the contractors and their friends to make an experimental excursion along the line. At Knott Mill the party including John Brogden boarded a train which consisted of engine and tender and two first class carriages, plus one third class covered carriage containing the Stretford Temperance Band which tunefully accompanied them through the rural pastures of Stretford and Sale on the way to Altrincham. The Manchester Courier for the 30th May 1849 wrote:–
"Many people collected along the line to watch it pass . . . and on arrival at Sale the work people, wrights, builders, smiths etc. turned out en masse and cheered lustily amidst the firing of canon and other demonstrations of welcome delight."

It is interesting to note that the same newspaper wrote a truly prophetic piece at this time:–
"There can be no question, we think that when the Altrincham Railway is opened, the number of houses in Altrincham, Bowdon, Timperley, Stretford, Ashton-on-Mersey and the other towns along the line will be greatly increased, in consequence of the great facility of transit which the railway will afford to the public."

As the years went by they were proved to be quite correct for the population of Sale alone more than tripled from this date to the end of the century.

When the railway was opened in 1849 not all the construction work was complete but this was rectified in the years that followed.

Originally the Sale Railway Station was merely one small hut, but by 1877 it had been altered to take the form shown in the photograph. The new station works were commenced in 1874 and included refurbishing the principal entrance shown here, protecting the front of the building with a large awning and constructing new windows and arches of parti-coloured bricks. The work cost £11,000; the station being designed by an architect called Mr. Woodhouse of Stafford. To complement these improvements the local nursery belonging to Birkenhead's supplied arrangements of plants for the entrance hall.

John Brogden

THE OLD BUS
SALE MOOR VILLAGE

Omnibus Services

The old bus pictured outside what is now the Temple Inn, Northenden Road, Sale, at the turn of the nineteenth century. At this period the property was listed in the local Slater's Directory as having been Nos. 103 and 105, fruiterers and beer retailers occupied by Jeremiah J. Wilkinson. Behind the bus is a boy carrying milk pails probably containing fresh milk from local herds, and behind him is the corner of a market garden belonging to Charles Braithwaite.

The omnibus above was a vehicle sometimes known as a station or hotel omnibus as it was often used to take people between these two establishments. They were often owned by private individuals but were also frequently used for hire for pleasure trips and moving goods from the railway station or town to their final destination. In many rural areas they were used as a form of local bus service even as late as the 1920's.

The design of the omnibus varied from being a four or six seater, with or without room for another passenger next to the driver. Windows could sometimes be located in the door at the rear as well as the sides and occasionally there was another one at the front as illustrated here. Similar to this one many had a firmly boarded roof surrounded by a protective rail to enable items of luggage to be carried on the roof leaving maximum space for passengers inside. The body of this type of omnibus generally had a cranked or 'U' shaped rear axle with the carriage suspension being by means of a semi-elliptical spring at the rear of each side of the back axle. Behind the front wheels were full elliptical springs which are just visible in this photograph.

Cross Street c 1900 *opposite page*

Another method of transport for those fortunate folk who had the means to hire or own these vehicles, was the landau. Pictured outside the building known today as No. 120 Cross Street, is a landau possibly waiting to go to a wedding, hence the white ribbons on the driver's whip and head of the horse. Behind the vehicle was the associated business of Robert Edward Jones, coach proprietor, and also Sutton & Co., carriers. Next door, nearly off the edge of the photograph was the tailoring business of John William Bradley.

This series of buildings is very interesting being the oldest in Sale and having the distinction of being among the first brick houses built in the north west of England. The property was probably built between 1660 and 1680 when decorative patterns in brickwork were very fashionable; hence the elaborate head moulds or 'eye-brows' over the window and door. These served the useful purpose of sheltering the windows from the rain water as it dripped off a flagged roof which possessed no gutters.

When this old farmhouse was built it is thought that the majority of the 600 residents of Sale and Ashton-upon-Mersey would have been living in timber framed houses with thatched roofs, but between 1680 and 1720 brick replaced oak timbers as the common building material. Many of the distinctively narrow bricks would have been locally made for many years and are still in evidence in some old property in the area.

The Pelican Hotel c 1900

Looking back along Washway Road, it shows in some respects the old world meeting the new in the form of the old wagonettes parked in front of the hotel and the new 'balloon car' or tram on the road. The 'balloon cars' ran from about 1906 to 1913 or 1914.

The horse drawn wagonettes developed from the middle of the nineteenth century when their popularity compelled the original much smaller vehicle to be expanded into the type shown here. They would have held sixteen or more passengers and were so high that entry onto the vehicle would have been at the back by means of a ladder. Again, as illustrated here, some versions were equipped with a framework over which could be placed a canvas cover if the weather became inclement. Alternatively if it was a warm summer's day the canvas could be drawn back for the passengers to enjoy the sunshine. For this reason and the fact they

could accommodate so many people they were very popular for visits to the countryside or other excursions.

Another interesting feature about the Pelican Hotel was its connection with the locally famous Pelican Mile race. During the nineteenth century many of the large houses in Sale kept horses and ponies, some of which were entered in this pony trotting race which covered the distance from Marsland Road, Sale, to the Pelican Hotel. During those days of course, a race along Washway Road would have been comparatively hazardless, being in an age before the proliferation of the motor vehicle.

Apparently one year a contestant in the race had a pony which could beat all others over a distance of seven furlongs but was incapable of staying the course for a whole mile. So the night before the race the owner hired two men to dig up one of the milestones along the route and move it a hundred yards nearer!

Sale Moor Village 1912.

By the time the photograph (left) was taken of the Sale Bridge to Legh Arms tramways extension, the track had been completed and was being tested though it still awaited the sanction of the Board of Trade before it could be officially opened. On 3rd July 1912 it was duly inspected and declared fit for public use the following day. It is quite surprising that the photographer was able to take this picture at all for June 1912 was one of the wettest months of the year, rain having been recorded every day of the month except two.

At either side of the tram, behind the people who had congregated to see the arrival of the first tram along Northenden Road, were the local shops advertising items such as granulated sugar at 1d a pound or margarine at 1/- a pound. Further down the road it was possible to rent a semi-detached house for about £25 a year or a much smaller property, for instance in James Street, off Northenden Road for about 5/6d a week. If one was affluent the Manchester Evening News was advertising gentlemen's cashmere suits for 42/- and wedding rings from 10/6d to £5. To put these prices in perspective the average clerk would only be earning in the region of £1 a week.

Northenden Road

A view (top right) of work under way to lay new tram lines along Northenden Road in March 1912. By May the route was nearing completion and by mid June it was finished and awaiting its first tramcar.

First Tram to Timperley, August 15, 1906.

This picture must have been taken during a private trip for local dignitaries as the Altrincham Guardian reported that the route opened on Friday, August 17th when the new tramway was officially extended from the Sale area to West Timperley. The tramcars were patronized by both country people sampling the delights of the city of Manchester and city folk wishing to spend a few hours in the countryside of Sale and Timperley. Most days the journey from Piccadilly to West Timperley took about fifty minutes with only an interval of seven and a half minutes between any two of the fourteen vehicles that travelled this route.

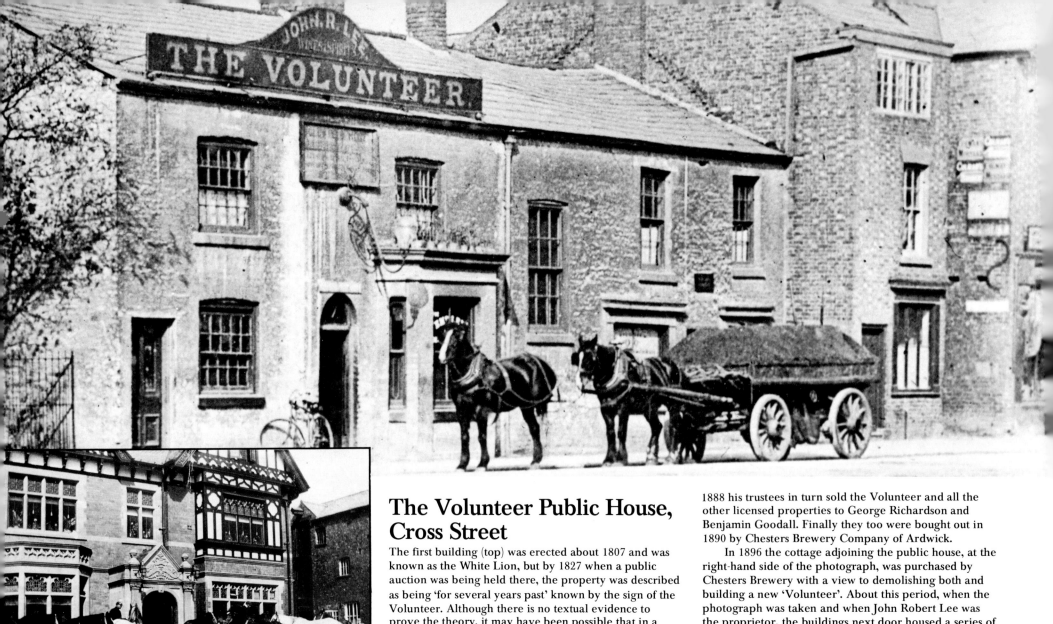

The Volunteer Public House, Cross Street

The first building (top) was erected about 1807 and was known as the White Lion, but by 1827 when a public auction was being held there, the property was described as being 'for several years past' known by the sign of the Volunteer. Although there is no textual evidence to prove the theory, it may have been possible that in a period of intense patriotism it was decided to change the name of one of the local public houses to commemorate the local defence unit – the Ashton-upon-Mersey-cum-Sale Loyal Volunteers who were mustered in 1803 to cope with a possible invasion by Napoleon; hence the Sale Volunteer.

However, in 1865 the property was purchased by a Mr. John Astle Kelsall, a brewer of Altrincham but in 1888 his trustees in turn sold the Volunteer and all the other licensed properties to George Richardson and Benjamin Goodall. Finally they too were bought out in 1890 by Chesters Brewery Company of Ardwick.

In 1896 the cottage adjoining the public house, at the right-hand side of the photograph, was purchased by Chesters Brewery with a view to demolishing both and building a new 'Volunteer'. About this period, when the photograph was taken and when John Robert Lee was the proprietor, the buildings next door housed a series of small traders including a sadler's, dressmaker's, grocer's and tripe dealer's and butcher's shop. The reconstruction of the public house swept away most of these premises and in 1898 the new Volunteer Hotel was opened. The second photograph (left) taken in 1924 shows the new Volunteer. To the right of the public house was a hay loft, later converted into a grocer's shop and currently the site of a new block of offices.

The Nag's Head c1900

It was situated at the corner of Wythenshawe Road and Northenden Road. Constructed in either the late eighteenth century or early nineteenth century, it was not built as a public house, though it assumed this function in 1869. At some period in its history it was extended by the addition of the right-hand section shown in the photograph, though both end sections have since been demolished leaving what is probably the original building in the middle. Today it can still be seen though it has reverted to being residential property once more.

At the time of this picture it had three rooms downstairs which were used for drinking purposes but had little accommodation for the licensee and his family, as even the kitchen was used as part of the drinking rooms. At the back was a covered yard which was used as a scullery and wash-house, as this was the only area with a water supply – factors which helped contribute towards its closure as a public house.

By 1912 the licensing authorities began to closely examine the premises and as a result considered that the area already had sufficient public houses with the old Lindow Tavern only a few yards away, likewise the Carters' Arms and also one beer off-licence, with all these premises having better accommodation and sanitation than the Nag's Head Inn. Accordingly at a meeting of the Licensing sessions held at Altrincham Police Court the chairman and the Bench considered all these matters and further evidence suggested that business was not as good as it could have been. However, a Mr. Hockin speaking on behalf of the tenant Joseph Massey said that they considered trade to be quite good with consumption of beer and cider being in the range of four or five barrels and 12 or 13 dozen bottles a week. Finally the licence was withdrawn and the building ceased to be a public house.

The Bulls Head c1870

The earliest mention of the existence of the inn was in 1830 when it took the form of a low terraced building as shown here. This photograph was probably taken sometime during the 1870's before it was demolished to make way for the present Victorian structure built in 1879. At this period School Road, at the right-hand side of the public house, was only a very narrow lane at the junction with Cross Street and the Sale Local Board was anxious to widen the thoroughfare. This was part of a nationwide movement promoted by the Public Health Acts to improve roads, drainage and sewage facilities

The Bull's Head

The present Bulls Head which was built in 1879.

generally. In consequence the local authority bought part of the Bull's Head property, which was then demolished. School Road was widened and a new public house built which now came under the auspices of the local brewery company of George Hardy, later taken over by Bass Charrington.

In the 1890's when Tom Bumby was the proprietor of the Bull's Head, he was well known for providing a free breakfast each morning for about fifty poor children of the district; often giving them new clogs or clothes as well if their old ones had worn out. The money to finance this scheme was provided by the hotel patrons and sometimes by outside benefaction.

Sale Carnival

At one time Sale held a regular carnival as a means of acquiring extra funds for the Sale & Brooklands Hospital and the Ashton Nursing Home. The first carnival was held in 1921 and over the years up to the early 1930's, when it ceased altogether, managed to collect £8,000 for these establishments. Its processions were regularly watched by huge crowds while a corps of collectors would mingle with the spectators collecting donations for the hospitals. Many local traders decorated their premises and the streets would be hung with festoons and flags as revealed in the parade photograph of the old cars moving along School Road in the direction of the Railway Station.

Most years the procession would commence in Ashton Park at about 2.00 p.m. and gradually wind its way along Dumber Lane, Park Road, Ashton Lane, School Road and Northenden Road eventually ending in Broad Road and turning into Sale Park where the various participants, many of whom wore fancy dress, would be judged in a competition. In 1925 the procession of decorated lorries, comic characters, troupes of dancers and jazz bands was estimated to be about 1½ miles long and included such groups as the Dark Town Jazz Minstrels illustrated in the photograph of the group of people on the float outside the Carters Arms. As a jazz band they were very successful, often winning prizes for their performances. One year, when they were competing with other bands in the Sale Park on carnival day, they borrowed twenty pigeons which they secreted beneath their coats. They then struck up the number 'When the love bird leaves the nest', opened their jackets and out flew the birds.

During these years rose queens were very popular and Sale was no exception. In 1931 Miss Ethel Stott became the Carnival Rose Queen, pictured here in an open carriage covered with flowers shaded from lemon to flame. In fact the only sombre note of the day was when the Rose Queen laid a wreath of roses at the base of the War Memorial before continuing to the Sale Park.

By 1931 the great economic depression had hit the country and there was a feeling that many people could not support the attractions as well as they had done in previous years. Despite this and other problems the procession and competitions in the park were still held that year and were reported in the local newspaper as having included numerous costumed characters dressed as red Indians, convicts, bottle-fed heavyweight babies, a star clad Bacchus and a lampshade. Festivities continued in the park with tableaux of horse drawn vehicles, side shows, hoop-la and pie stalls for those who could afford them, but times were changing and the 1930's saw the end of the carnival.

Boer War Celebrations

These photographs depict scenes from the celebrations held at the end of the Boer War in 1902. The idea of having an ox roast in Sale was attributed to a Mr. T. Wallis of Cross Street, Ashton, whose idea was soon taken up by a number of local tradesmen who decided to invite all the school children in the neighbourhood to participate in a festive meal to be held in June.

Celebrations took place off Glebelands Road in a field lent by Mr. Howarth Bailey. Mr. T. Robinson, a butcher of Cross Street made his contribution by purchasing an ox on behalf of the Celebration Committee and placing it in one of his own decorated floats as shown. The unfortunate animal was then paraded through the streets of Sale and Ashton to the accompaniment of the Ashton-on-Mersey Band. The resulting procession was probably unique in the annals of the district for as well as the ox, five of the celebrated performing elephants which had belonged to a travelling show called the 'Savage South Africa Show' were borrowed for the parade. Hundreds of people watched the procession as it visited Ashton Village, School Road and Northenden Road on its way to Sale Moor and then Dane Road and Cross Street. It was headed by a vehicle containing Mr. Fred Vickers the chairman of the Celebration Committee, Mr. Rooney the secretary and Mr. J. Hepplethwaite, followed by the band, the ox in the float and of course the elephants. Along the route youths with collecting boxes appealed to the public to contribute towards the funds required for the festivities, anything in excess to be divided between the Sale and Ashton District's Nursing Funds.

The day before the festivities the process of roasting the ox was started in the large open furnace shown here. The carcass was held in position by a circular bar of iron crossing the entire width of the fire and resting on the brick walls at either side. It required the efforts of about twelve men to raise the carcass into position and commence the roasting at 7.45 p.m. on the night before the celebrations. A cog wheel fixed to one end of the apparatus was worked alternately by two men until the roasting was complete at 11.00 a.m. the following morning. In the meantime a long rectangular pan had been placed beneath the roast to catch the scalding fat which was then used for basting by means of two long handled ladles.

Mr. Henry V. Kilvert of 'Kilvert's lard' fame cut the first slice of meat before the rest of the ox was carved and distributed to about 2,000 local school children who each received a slice of bread and a piece of beef. By the evening several thousand people had joined in the celebrations, the Ashton-on-Mersey Band played and people danced until it was dark.

Sale Moor Cricket & Hockey Club Fete

(Right) A scene of a typical English summer fete just after the Edwardian era and before the conflagration of World War I. The Sale Moor Cricket & Hockey Club held their fete in the grounds on Baguley Road and in July 1912 when this picture was taken, can be seen assembling round the refreshment tents. During the opening ceremony Mr. E. F. Stockton, the captain of the Cricket Club commented on the subject of cricket as being a game which 'was one of the finest possible for strengthening the characters of those participating'.

The events included many entertainments featuring selections of popular songs played by the Heyrod Street Old Boys Military Band, performances by the Frivolities Concert Party and gymnastic displays by members of the Sale St. Anne's Brotherhood Social Club. Fancy costume dancing was given by Miss Eileen Walley and a feature of old English sports provided a great attraction so that by the end of the day the fete had produced a profit of £20.

Chapel Road

A few minutes relaxation for local children and a few adults, while they watched a puppet show at the top of Chapel Road near its junction with Cross Street. At the right-hand side one can see the Volunteer Public House and behind the trees the spire of the Ashton-on-Mersey United Reformed Church peeps out. Taken in about 1900 the photograph shows how quiet the roads must have been before the age when motor vehicles began to dominate this route.

Worthington Park

Opened in the same year as the Relief of Mafeking, Sale Park or Worthington Park was formally opened on 30th June 1900. In 1897 the Sale Council had decided to appoint a committee to consider ways of commemorating Queen Victoria's long reign. It was eventually recommended that an open space should be purchased at the expense of the local ratepayers, who immediately called a meeting and declined the scheme. But during this period an anonymous benefactor appeared who donated £7,200 for the purchase of the land. Unfortunately the ratepayers' meetings were still the scene of heated argument as they would still be faced with the bill for fencing and landscaping; part of a

project which they termed as being 'absolutely unnecessary'.

However, the scheme went ahead and a short time before the grand opening it became known that Mrs. Worthington of Sale Lodge, the widow of the late Mr. James Worthington who had been a member of the Sale Local Board, had been the anonymous donor. The photograph shows the opening of the park, an occasion on which about 2,500 local Sunday School children were invited to attend and each provided with a small commemorative medal of the event. The opening ceremony began at 4.00 p.m. when Mrs. Worthington was greeted by the Chairman of the Council, Mr. John Morley, and presented with a golden key to open the park gates.

They then proceeded to the platform, where various speeches were made and the park declared officially open as a monument to the spirit of the Victorian age.

The 16½ acre park was designed and laid out by the local engineer and surveyor Mr. A. G. McBeath, while the buildings were designed by his architect son Mr. Robert J. McBeath. Various local figures either contributed to the funds or donated gifts such as a Mrs. Grimshaw who gave the park its carved stone lion and several vases. In those days the park was somewhat different from today having a full-time park keeper's lodge, spacious summer houses, a well used band stand and an ornamental lake.

King George V Coronation Celebrations

In June 1911 Sale, in common with many other towns, celebrated the coronation of King George V. The rejoicing began at 11.00 a.m. with thanksgiving services in the various churches, and continued in the afternoon with processions of Sunday School children.

(Left) Pictured at the top of School Road in the area of the present cenotaph, is Mr. Samuel Garnet Harris with his son Samuel P. Harris who wore the fancy dress costume of John Bull and rode a pony. Years later the little boy became one of the community's well known councillors, becoming Mayor of Sale in 1961–62.

The procession of Sale Sunday schools, of which this photograph shows but a small corner, was an imposing event including some 3,000 people. Some of the schools did their best to create an atmosphere of a pageant with children carrying bouquets and shepherd's crooks dressed with flowers and ribbons. Master Samuel P. Harris represented the Trinity Wesleyan school and accompanied other children dressed as milk maids, sailors and fairy tale characters.

The procession was led by the Altrincham Borough Band through the streets to Sale Park. Here everyone joined in the National Anthem, after which an oak tree was planted in commemoration of the event, the children watched Punch & Judy shows and the band played selections of popular tunes. Later in the afternoon the children returned to their respective Sunday schools where they were entertained to tea and sent home with a souvenir mug of the occasion. In the evening the adults culminated the celebrations with a display of fireworks at the Sale and Ashton-on-Mersey Conservative Club.

Market Gardening & Farming

If one studies the 1870's edition of the Ordnance Survey maps of Sale one can see a preponderance of glasshouses and smallholdings, many of which were market gardens catering for the Manchester market as well as local trade. In many places in Sale the soil was particularly fertile and had a high water table producing ideal conditions for the cultivation of flowers and vegetables.

By the early years of the twentieth century the locality was growing a wide variety of produce. Vegetables included cauliflowers, broccoli, cabbages, potatoes and carrots as well as the ever popular salad crops of tomatoes, lettuce and cucumber. Rhubarb was also grown in large quantities and forced in special 40 feet long, windowless rhubarb sheds which had wide sloping roofs covered with roofing felt. Here the crop was harvested in February or in colder years in March, then boxed and then taken to market. Timperley was also another famous area for rhubarb, giving its name to the variety 'Timperley Early'.

Flowers too were commercially grown, including lilies, chrysanthemums, dahlias, asters and the ever popular sweet peas, though marguerites and various species of dianthus were also favourites. In the latter category the old-fashioned pinks were in steady demand, including the varieties Mrs. Sinkins and Mrs. Clibran.

These were the days before the widespread use of artificial fertilizers when one of the basic ways of keeping the land in 'good heart' was by the use of manure. Many of the market gardeners would take their produce to market in Manchester and return with a load of manure rather than an empty cart. One of the favourite stopping places was the Midland Hotel where the empty vehicle could be loaded with horse manure from their stables. When the load of manure had been purchased it was not unknown for the occasional bit of bartering to take place; the market gardener offering a few young cabbages in exchange for a yard brush. Apart from manure, blood and bonemeal were also used on the land and occasionally 'Clay's Fertilizer' was used to speed up growth.

The Garner Family lived at New Farm on Washway Road.
Above: John Arthur Garner at the back of the farm with Prince.
Opposite: Cauliflowers loaded for Smithfield Market, Manchester.
They would be sold by the Garners for about ½d each, at their own
stall at Smithfield. Local shopkeepers would buy from them directly.
Below right: Henry Brownhill's shop opposite the Legh Arms Hotel
in Sale Moor.

Opposite page: Woodheys Farm, Harboro Rd, Ashton-upon-Mersey.
The photographs were taken around 1925. The farm covered 30 acres
in the area which is now Cecil Avenue.

Ashton-upon-Mersey c1910

The fountain at the junction of Ashton Lane with Moss Lane and Barkers Lane in the days when it was still used as a water trough for passing horses before the road junction was altered to accommodate modern traffic. It was built as the result of the generosity of the local Member of Parliament, Sir William Cunliffe Brooks who in the closing decades of the nineteenth century was responsible for donating the land upon which the church of St. Mary Magdalene was built and adding the tower and lych gate to St. Martin's church amongst various other acts of munificence.

Green Lane, Ashton-upon-Mersey, c1900

The building with the clock tower was the old St. Martin's School in the days when it was still used for educational purposes.

The junction of Chapel Road and School Road in 1932

This was the corner of Sale Town Hall before it was extended and Chapel Road widened. Next door Fowler & Co., Scientific Instrument Makers, occupied a building that had originally been the site of the old Congregational Chapel which in turn had been purchased in 1851 for use as a Wesley Methodist Chapel. At a later date it became the Sale Institute when it would resound with the songs of many a theatrical performance. By 1919 it was taken over by Fowler & Co. who carried out various alterations. At one time this corner was also the site of the Sale Market, illustrated elsewhere in this collection. Behind Fowler's the row of terraced houses opposite the Bridgewater Canal is now a car park.

Jackson's Boat c1880

Although included in this selection of photographs, at the time of writing (1983) the Bridge Inn at Jackson's Boat while appearing to be on the Sale side of the River Mersey is actually within the Manchester city boundaries. Jackson's Boat originally acquired its name from a local farmer named Jackson who cultivated a large tract of land in this vicinity and who regularly ferried people across the river by means of a boat for which he charged a small fee. By 1814 when the grounds and property were advertised as being for sale this piece of land was described as "Jackson's of the Boat" or the "Boat House". Eventually the ferry service was replaced by a wooden footbridge in 1816 but this was unfortunately washed away in a heavy storm and was rebuilt in 1881 in the form of an iron girder bridge. At this period in its history people still had to pay a fee to cross the river though it was now in the form of a bridge toll which amounted to one halfpenny per person on foot or a penny if one had a bicycle. This system was not abolished until the end of the 1940's when Manchester Corporation purchased the bridge and freed the licensee of the public house from the onerous task of collecting the tolls.

The present inn was once the site of an old wood and planter house but this was demolished to make way at the end of the eighteenth century for the inn shown here. Over the years various articles have been written about its romantic associations with the days of the Manchester Jacobites when it is said that men including Colonel Townley of the Manchester regiment and the famous Dr. John Byrom used to meet regularly with men of a similar persuasion to drink the health of the King.

Cornfield opposite the old Sale Library, c1890's *(above left)*

This cornfield now occupies the corner site of a row of terraced houses in Tatton Road which in turn led on to the old Savoy Cinema building in Ashfield Road and the houses at the corner of Claremont Road. At the time of the photograph the building in the middle of the picture was the Police Station with the Technical School and Sale Library at the right-hand side.

The junction of Dane Road and Cross Street, c1900 *(above right)*

Some of the terraced property in the background is still standing though the other buildings on Cross Street were demolished and the main road widened in 1959/60. The site on the right-hand side now houses the Department of Health and Social Security office while the cottages on the left-hand side gave way to lawns and modern business premises.

Glebelands Road, c1900 *(right)*